WE GO ECO

AF904428

THE HOMES WE BUILD

WRITTEN BY KATIE WOOLLEY

ILLUSTRATED BY SOPHIE FOSTER

WINDMILL BOOKS

Published in 2027 by Windmill Books,
an Imprint of Rosen Publishing
2544 Clinton St.
Buffalo, NY 14224

First published in Great Britain in 2023 by Hodder and Stoughton
Copyright © Hodder and Stoughton, 2023

Author: Katie Woolley
Illustrators: Sophie Foster and Hannah Wood
In-House Editor: Melanie Palmer
Designer: Lisa Peacock

Picture credits:
Simon Marina/AFP/Getty Images: 28, 29.

Cataloging-in-Publication Data
Names: Woolley, Katie, author. | Foster, Sophie, illustrator.
Title: The homes we build / by Katie Woolley, illustrated by Sophie Foster.
Description: Buffalo, NY : Windmill Books, an imprint of Rosen Publishing, 2027. |
Series: We go eco | Includes glossary and index.
Identifiers: ISBN 9781725398573 (pbk.) | ISBN 9781725398580 (library bound) | ISBN 9781725398597 (ebook)
Subjects: LCSH: Dwellings--Juvenile literature. | Ecological houses--Juvenile literature. | Architecture, Domestic--Environmental aspects--Juvenile literature. | Sustainable architecture--Juvenile literature.
Classification: LCC GT172.W66 2027 | DDC 392.36--dc23

All rights reserved.

All facts and statistics were up to date at the time of press.
Every attempt has been made to clear copyright.
Should there be any inadvertent omission please apply to the publisher for rectification.

No part of this book may be reproduced in any form without permission
in writing from the publisher, except by a reviewer.

Printed in China

CPSIA Compliance Information: Batch #QS27WM
For Further Information contact Rosen Publishing at 1-800-237-9932

Find us on

CONTENTS

WHAT IS A HOME?

A home is a house, an apartment, a building, or another place where people live.

hut

apartment

houseboat

igloo

A house often has walls, a roof, windows, and doors. We need building materials to build a house. These include bricks, stones, steel, wood, or ice.

Houses are built from materials that can be transported to the building site. There are lots of different ways to build a house.

DIFFERENT HOMES

In the past, houses were built using materials that people could find easily nearby.

There was lots of wood in forests, so houses were often made from wood, straw, and mud.

Later on, houses were built from human-made materials, such as brick and glass.

Today, houses are made from all sorts of materials. You can still live in a cottage with a thatched roof made of reeds and straw. But it is possible to live in a home that is built using lots of different materials too.

BUILDING MATERIALS

Today, it is easy to transport different materials long distances. This makes house building easier. Builders don't need to just use local materials anymore.

But building houses has a big impact on the planet. Clearing land to build houses can destroy habitats and harm wildlife. The building process and the materials that are used produce greenhouses gases, pollution, and waste.

HOUSES AND CLIMATE CHANGE

Modern houses are often made from concrete. Concrete is made by mixing cement with sand, gravel, and water.

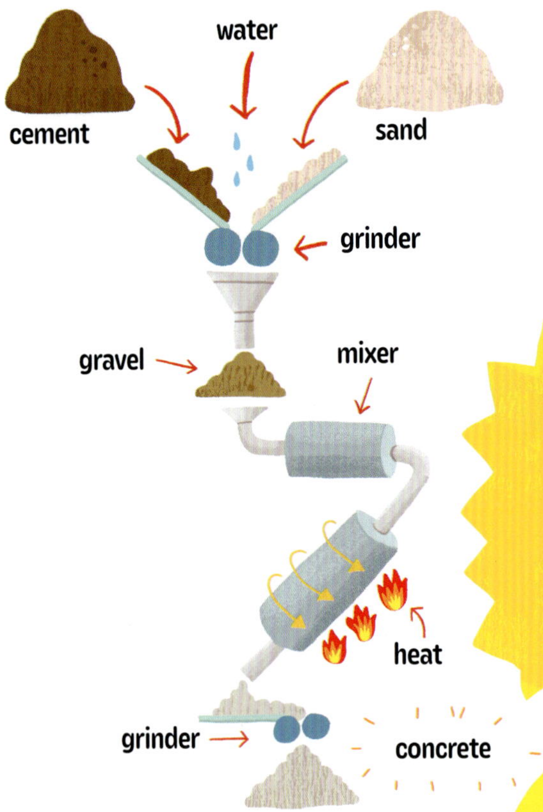

To make concrete, the mixture is heated. This process makes a lot of carbon dixoide.

Carbon dixoide is a greenhouse gas. It goes in the air and traps the sun's heat.

Eco-Tip
Talk with your family and friends and find out what your house is made from.

Steel is another strong building material. A fossil fuel called coal is burned in a factory to make steel. This process also sends heat and harmful gases into the atmosphere.

When heat cannot escape, Earth gets hotter and hotter. This is called global warming, and it is causing climate change.

CONCRETE AND STEEL

Concrete absorbs heat from the sun but not rainwater. Places with lots of concrete, such as cities, can become very hot. The use of concrete to build homes can also cause more floods, as rainwater has nowhere to go.

- Recycle and reuse concrete when making a new house.

- Find ways to save energy and use more recycled materials in our homes.

- Find a different way to make steel that does not burn fossil fuels.

- Plant trees on streets with lots of concrete houses. The trees help soak up water. This reduces flooding.

BUILDING A HOUSE TODAY

Today, architects and builders need to think about the planet when they build a home.

Green roofs can absorb the sun's heat and make homes for wildlife.

Solar panels turn the sun's heat into energy for use in the home.

A rain barrel can collect rainwater to water garden plants.

Insulated walls and floors keep houses warm in the winter and cool in the summer.

Eco-friendly building materials can help protect the planet.

- What kinds of windows will keep the heat in? ☑
- What will the walls be made of? ☑
- How will the home be heated? ☑
- What materials are most eco-friendly? ☑
- How will the home be insulated to keep it warm? ☑
- Where will the household trash go? ☑

Eco-Tip
Learn more about what it takes to be an architect or builder.

ECO-FRIENDLY MATERIALS

One way to make houses more eco friendly is to use natural materials. Some houses around the world use bamboo sticks or coconut trees.

Some houses use both natural materials and human-made ones. Builders can add bamboo fibers to concrete to use less concrete.

Green roofs on the top of a house can absorb rainwater and reduce air pollution.

In a village in Guatemala, a woman built her house using plastic bottles filled with plastic waste. These are called "eco-blocks."

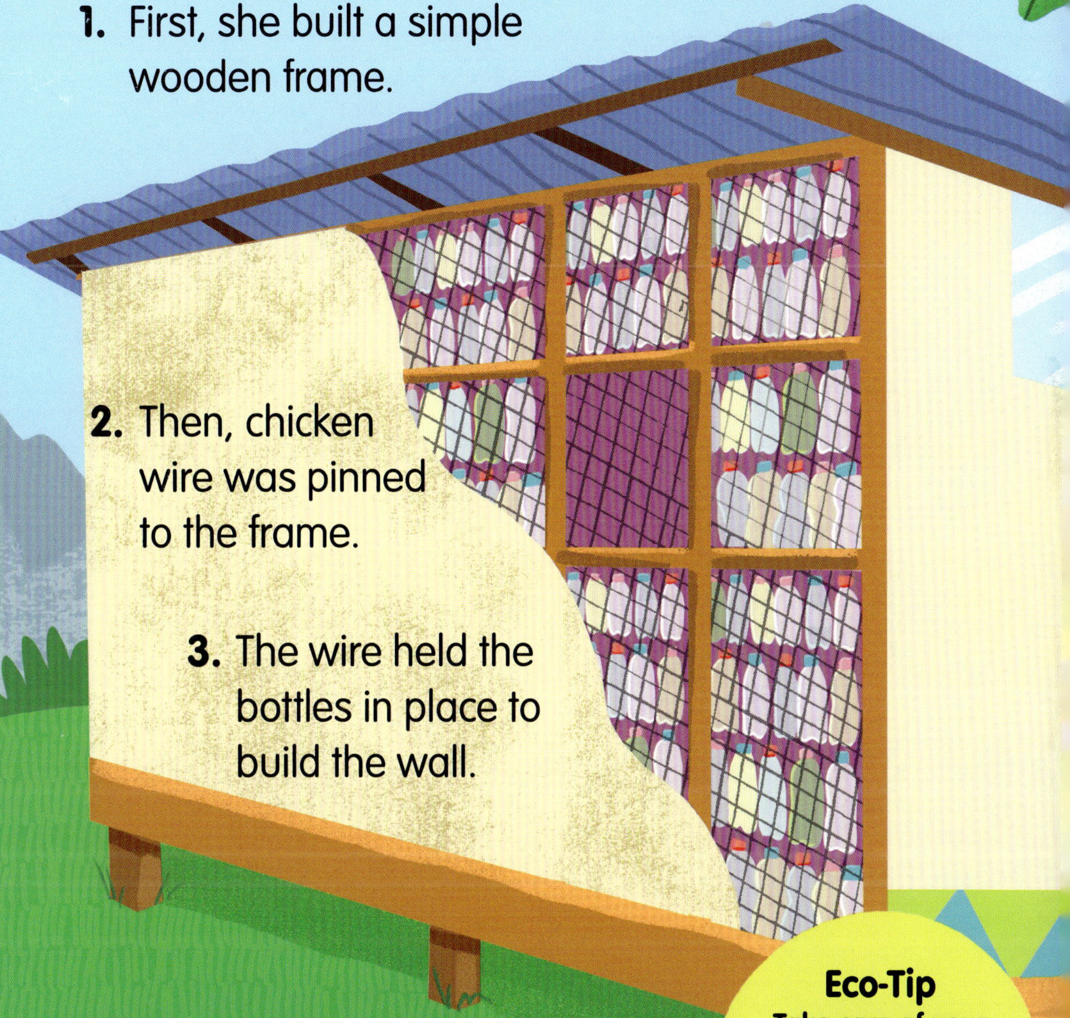

1. First, she built a simple wooden frame.

2. Then, chicken wire was pinned to the frame.

3. The wire held the bottles in place to build the wall.

4. The walls were then covered to make them very strong.

Eco-Tip

Take care of your neighborhood! Why not organize an afternoon of cleaning up trash?

OLD HOMES

Not all houses are new. A lot of old homes are not very eco friendly. But there are things we can do to make all homes better for the planet.

- Solar panels on the roof can help generate some of the electricity and hot water that is used by people in a house.

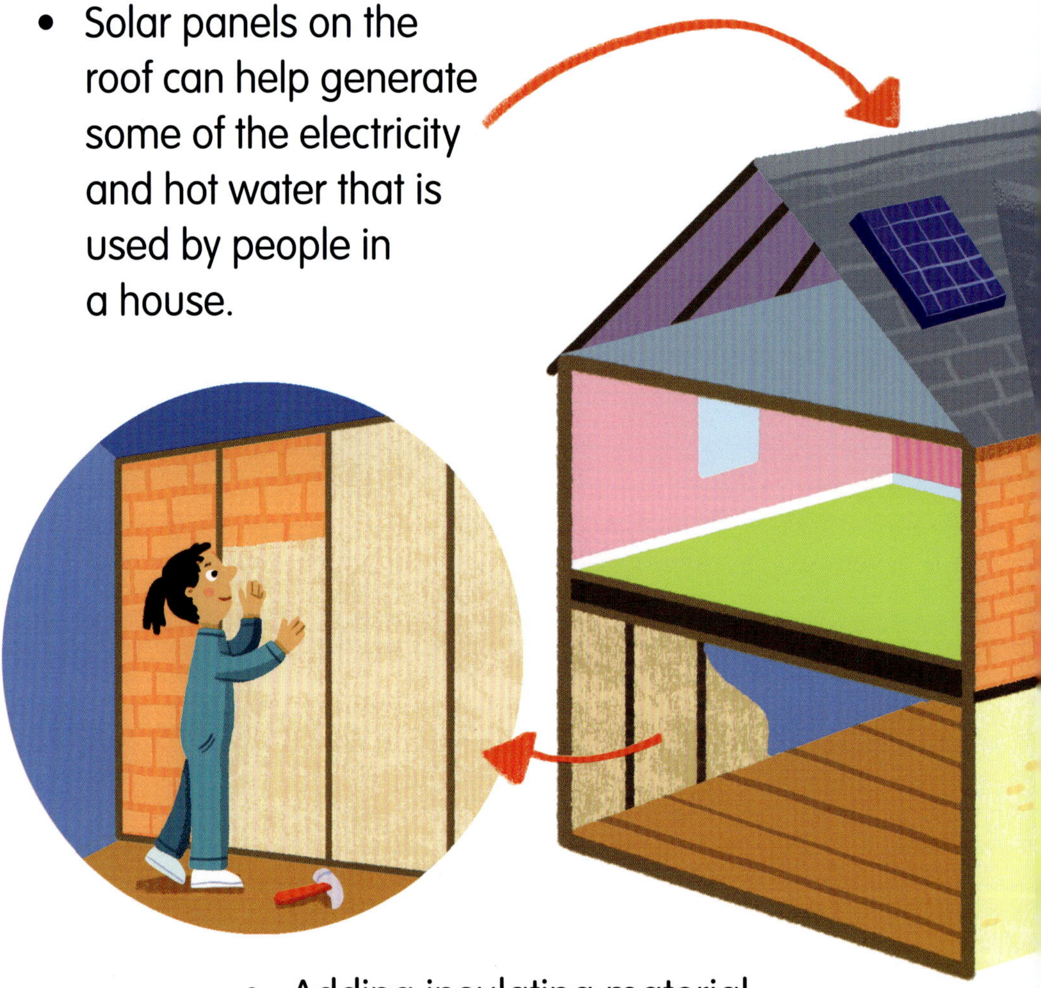

- Adding insulating material to walls can stop the flow of heat in and out.

- Growing plants on roofs and walls keeps houses cool in the summer and helps stop heat from escaping the house in winter months.

- Windows can be changed to fit better and have more than one layer of glass. This can stop heat from escaping.

ECO-TIP
Grow your own garden on a windowsill. You don't need lots of room to add some green space.

INSIDE OUR HOMES

Our homes use a lot of energy. We need energy to light up the rooms. We use energy to keep our homes warm in the winter and cool in the summer.

We also need electrical energy to power our electrical devices, such as computers, lights, and fans.

All this energy use adds up. It means the homes we live in aren't always very eco friendly. But you don't have to build a new house to make your home better for the planet. Here are some tips to be more "eco" at home:

- Turn off devices and lights when they are not in use.

- Use LED light bulbs that use less energy.

- Curtains, rugs, and carpets can help insulate your home.

ECO-TIP
You can take quicker showers to save energy and water. You can also turn off the water while brushing your teeth!

OUTSIDE OUR HOMES

There are things that we can do outside our homes too.

If you do have outdoor space, you could use a rain barrel to collect rainwater.

You don't have to have a big garden to bring nature into your home. Plant seeds in a pot or egg carton and create a small garden for local wildlife.

Eco-Tip
Use the water in your rain barrel to give your garden a drink on dry, sunny days.

Think about how you get to and from your home. More and more people are changing to electric cars.

WHAT CAN WE DO AT HOME?

The trash in our homes adds up! Everything we buy is made using energy and materials. Reducing the amount of new things we buy helps the planet.

People are also looking at different ways to recycle our waste. For example, it is possible to buy clothes made from old plastic bottles.

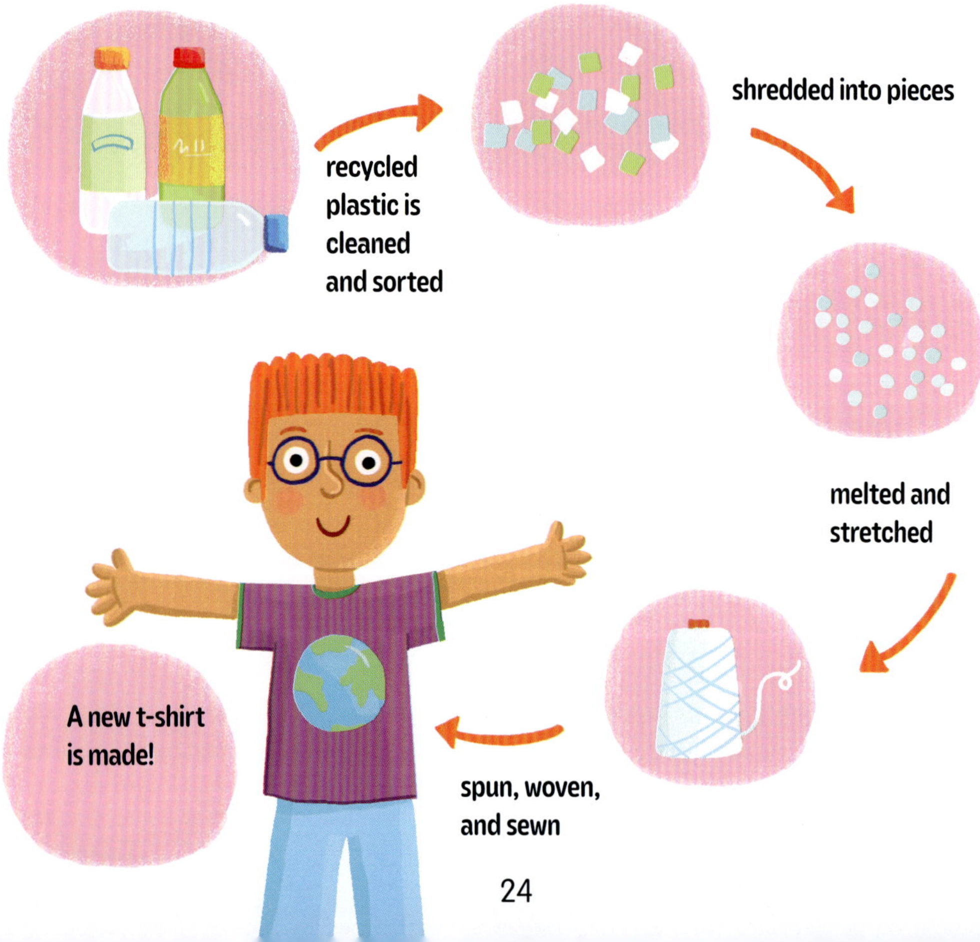

It's possible to turn old bottle corks into cork flooring for a home.

Recycled glass can be turned into new bathroom tiles or kitchen countertops.

You can even use a trash sorting system in your house that is made from recycled plastic!

ECO-TIP

Find out how to turn an old t-shirt into a reusable shopping bag.

BECOME AN ECO WARRIOR

A lot of our things end up in a landfill or in the ocean when we're done using them. These things take a long time to break down. They can harm habitats too. Instead of throwing things away it's time to Go Eco!

- Give old clothes to someone else who can still use them.

- Look through your trash and see if you can use it to make something new. For example, you can use old paper towel rolls to make some crafts.

- Try not to use single-use items, such as cups. Use reusable ones instead.

- Reduce the food you buy that is wrapped in plastic packaging. This means less plastic waste ends up in the ocean.

EARTH ACTIVIST: NZAMBI MATEE

Nzambi Matee grew up in Kenya, which is in Africa. There, she saw how hard it was for people to build a decent home. She set out to change that.

Nzambi founded a company that turns plastic waste into bricks that are stronger than concrete! They are cheap to make and easy to use. This means many eco-friendly homes can be built to protect the people of Kenya.

Her company has also given jobs to trash collectors, women, and young people in the area.

GLOSSARY

Absorb take in or soak up

Architect someone who designs buildings

Climate change the long-term changes in Earth's temperature

Concrete a material used in the building of many homes, offices, and schools

Eco-friendly material a material that is designed to have little or no harmful effect on the planet

Environment the area in which a person, animal, and plant lives

Fossil fuel a fuel, such as oil, coal, and gas, made from the remains of things that lived long ago

Greenhouse gas one of the gases in Earth's atmosphere that traps heat

Habitat the natural home or environment of an animal or plant

Pollution when gases, smoke, or other harmful materials are released into the air, water, or land, causing harm to people, plants, and animals

Thatched roof a traditional way to build a roof that uses straw to create a covering

Transported taken or carried from one place to another

INDEX